Old Testament
Reading Plan & Workbook

Level I
Middle School

Laura R. Langhoff Arndt

Cover Images by Sweet Publishing/freeBibleimages.org

The materials in this book are for educational purposes only. For more information contact the author at:

www.carpentersministrytoolbox.com

CreateSpace with Carpenter's Ministry Press

ISBN: 0692255761
ISBN-13: 978-0692255766

DEDICATION

To all the teachers of the faith who realize that the truth lies in the
Word of God and there alone.

And to my husband, Kevin, who is my constant support and keeps me on the biblical straight and narrow.

All Scripture is breathed out by God and profitable for teaching, for reproof, for correction, and for training in
righteousness, that the man of God may be competent, equipped for every good work.
2 Timothy 3:16-17 ESV

INTRODUCTION

"Biblical literacy is neither a current reality nor a goal in the U.S." (The Barna Group, www.barna.org) Most churches don't require Bible reading other than certain chosen passages to support a story or topic being studied. What many Christians believe about the Bible and their faith is completely misguided. The problem stems from:

1) **Not really knowing what the Bible says.** Christians are creating their own version of Christianity based on what they want to believe is true as opposed to what the Bible teaches. Barna's research suggests that this practice takes effect in the early teenage years and that by the time most kids reach the age of 14 they think they know everything about the Bible and don't need to read it anymore.

2) **Reading out of context.** One of the things missing from confirmation education is the expectation to read the Bible in more than short sections or specifically chosen verses. Barna says, "Bible reading has become the religious equivalent of sound-bite journalism." If it fits on a coffee cup and they agree with it then they accept it. As a result of this practice, students go through confirmation without understanding the fundamental themes and have little interest in deepening their knowledge of the Bible or its author.

Students need to know what the Bible says before they can truly think about it. They need to understand it in context to grasp God's work and his relationship with His people, them. One challenge with the Old Testament is that it is long and contains some difficult books for middle school students to read. This program is developed from the *70 Most Important Events in the Bible.*

Level I

Until this point, students have heard and talked about various stories in Sunday School but have never had the opportunity to read about them themselves, or to connect them to the greater picture and relationship God had/has with His people. The Level I course, the *Old Testament Bible Reading Plan* for middle school/confirmation, is a one year, 33 week reading plan with comprehension questions, or is for the person who has not yet read the Bible. The questions are primarily plot oriented in order to give students an overall understanding of the story of God's Old Testament people. Students should be able to relate the stories back to the educator with accuracy and be able to tell what God is doing and what the people are doing, as well as apply what they know about them in different ways. **The questions are not meant to be all encompassing or theologically comprehensive in nature. They are meant to get students thinking about what they are reading and what's happening in each account.** Greater discussion can and should be had with the pastor or confirmation educator regarding more theological or doctrinal issues as the students read.

Level II

At this point, students should have read Level I and have a basic understanding of the Old Testament. High school students are more advanced with regard to cognitive development so the Level II questions are deeper and encourage students to think about more than just the plot now that they are more familiar with the ongoing story. They encourage students to think more deeply about what they've read and how it relates to their world. The questions are still not doctrinal or theologically comprehensive in nature as those things should be discussed by the pastor or educator.

Answers

Answers are intentionally not included so that students feel free to share their thoughts, allowing leaders to discover what the students think or believe about what they've read. It will also enhance discussion and help leaders to know when students are misunderstanding what they're reading. If educators are unfamiliar with any particular reading they may read along with the students. Those questions that are plot oriented, are easy to answer when reading along with the students. Questions that require deeper or personal thoughts or opinions have no "right" answer.

FOR THE TEACHER
RECOMMENDED IMPLEMENTATION

1. **This program is not complete without discussion.** Middle school students often need help making connections and it's hard to tell what they do or do not understand unless you talk about it or have them interact with it in other ways. For an 1½ hour class, take at least 15 minutes of class time to discuss (not correct) their answers. Students should be able to relate the plot and facts of each account with accuracy. They may need guidance to connect how each reading relates to the past readings in this ongoing story. If you need to, add at least 15 minutes to the class session in order to add discussion time. That's how important it is in the learning process! (See Appendix D: The Art of Leading Discussion)

2. Expect more from your students! **Expect them to complete the work before they arrive each week.** Do not let students try to convince you there are too many questions even with other memory work. They have an entire week to complete the work and having homework such as this reinforces its importance to the parents. If parents complain, remind them that this is the most important thing they can do for their kids at this moment and for their future.

3. **Look over their answers each week** and give an ink stamp or a sticker to those who complete the work. Keep a check list or spreadsheet of those who are/are not completing the readings. It's important for students to know they will be held accountable for the work. If you don't take it seriously, they won't either.

4. **Ask questions** about or refer them back to previous readings to help them link everything together. This is a long and continuing story, not a bunch of disconnected stories with one main character.

5. **Remember the developmental level** of middle school students. Don't expect them to be able to rationalize, debate, or argue at an adult level. Their brains are just developing in that area and their logic may not always make sense.

6. **Correct them when they misunderstand what they've read.** Use this or a similar phrase often, "*Child's Name,* you had an interesting question/comment this week, let's talk about it." Comments such as that show students that you care about what they think and write, that you have a desire to answer all their questions, and gives them confidence to continue to question.

CONTENTS

STUDENT INSTRUCTIONS

✓ Always pray before reading the Bible. A possible prayer:

Open my heart and mind, Lord, to what you have to teach me through your Word today. May it stick with me, help me to understand you better, and bring me closer to you. Amen.

✓ Read through the whole reading once before you read the questions.

✓ Answer every question in your own words unless specifically asked to quote something.

✓ Write down anything that confuses you and ask a pastor, teacher, or parent to help you understand before, during, or after class. No question, curiosity, or concern should go unasked!

✓ Feel free to highlight or write anything that touches your heart or mind in your Bible.

PARENT INSTRUCTIONS

✓ Pray for your child(ren). Pray for their hearts and their minds to be open to what they read, hear, and learn throughout the process. Pray that God grow their faith and keep them close.

✓ Pray *with* your child(ren). It will have a huge impact on their prayer life and reinforce with them that personal prayer is important.

✓ Look at their answers to hold them accountable and encourage them of the importance of not rushing through it just to be done.

✓ Ask them about what they've read and what they find interesting about it and are learning from it. (You might want to read the passages yourself. ☺)

✓ Talk to them about your faith and about how having faith affects how you live.

✓ Be diligent and supportive in holding them accountable for their reading. Be sure they aren't rushing through it and are taking the time to think about their answers.

✓ Talk about what they're reading at the dinner table. It never hurts for siblings to participate and/or hear the discussion. Contact the pastor about anything that comes up that you aren't sure about.

✓ Aside from the Holy Spirit, PARENTS are a child's single greatest influence with regard to faith and whether or not it takes root in their lives.

WEEK 1: Where We Came From   Genesis 1 – 2

1. List the order in which God created everything.

2. What was the phrase God used after each day of creation?

3. How did God describe everything the He had made?

4. What do you think is the point of God creating the world?

5. God created us last and was very proud of us. We are the crowning achievement of His creation. What do you think that means for you?

6. Why do you think God created man/woman? Why do you think He created YOU?

7. Everyone needs a purpose. When God created Adam, what purpose did he give him?

8. Why do you think God didn't want them to eat of the tree of knowledge of good and evil?

9. Describe how God shows us He loves us throughout creation?

10. What does "bone of my bones and flesh of my flesh" tell you about the relationship between man and woman?

11. God made a point to tell us they felt no shame. What does *shame* mean?

12. Why do you think they should or should not feel shame?

13. What kinds of things in life today should make people feel shame?

What lessons can we learn from this reading for our personal faith and life?

WEEK 2: The Fall of Man… Into Trouble   Genesis 3 – 4

---

1. What words or phrases give you an idea of how God enjoyed spending time with His people? What did they do together?

2. What about the forbidden fruit made Eve want to eat it?

3. Who did Adam blame for eating the fruit? Who did Eve blame? What is your first instinct when somebody catches you doing something wrong?

4. What do you think entices us to do what God asks us not to do?

5. What did Adam and Eve receive from eating the forbidden fruit? What changed in them?

6. When God made it impossible for Adam and Eve to return to the garden, what was He protecting them from?

7. God knows everything. Why do you think he put the tree of knowledge of good and evil in the garden if he knew Adam and Eve would eat from it?

8. Just like Adam and Eve, we make choices to go against God's plan for us every day. What are some choices you make that take you further away from God?

9. What was the problem between Cain and Abel?

10. What was the consequence of Cain's behavior? How did God show that He still loved him?

11. From which of Adam's sons did Jesus come?

12. When you look around at the world today what evidence do you see that the world is broken by sin?

13. God's intention was that his creatures live in a relationship with Him. What changed that?

14. What does it mean for God's people and their lives that they will no longer live in the garden with Him?

What lessons can we learn from this reading for our personal faith and life?

WEEK 3: It Rained And Poured   **Genesis 6 – 9**

1. After the flood, God decided people would not live forever. How long would they live?

2. What was wrong with the people on earth?

3. What does *corrupt* mean?

4. This is the first time the word *covenant* is used in the Bible. What does *covenant* mean?

5. Covenant is used three times in this reading. Who is it between and what is this covenant?

6. What did God do to show that He hadn't given up completely on His people?

7. What was different about Noah (and his family)?

8. How long did Noah have to wait for the waters to recede?

9. What do you think happened to the raven?

10. Noah's first act after coming out of the ark was to build an altar. What is an altar?

11. Why did Noah need an altar? (What is its purpose?)

12. After getting off the ark, what did God tell Noah regarding the animals?

13. God's covenant was not just with Noah and his descendants. Who/what else?

14. Given the state of creation, what do you think would have happened if God had not destroyed the world at this time?

15. In what ways does God use the lives of people to further His plan of salvation?

16. What did Ham do that made his father so angry?

What lessons can we learn from this reading for our personal faith and life?

WEEK 4: How Far Will It Go?/Oh, Abram!   Genesis 10 – 12

1. Why do you think genealogies are in the Bible?

2. For what purpose were the people building a city and a tower?

3. What do you think is wrong with the people wanting to build a city with a tower that reaches to the heavens?

4. How did confusing their language solve the problem?

5. The Tower of Babel is a short reading. Why do you think it's important?

6. What did God ask of Abram?

7. What did God promise to Abram?

8. What did it mean that God will bless Abram and Abram will be a blessing; "all the people of the earth will be blessed" through him?

9. Why was Abram building altars to God?

10. God doesn't always lead us as clearly as He seemed to lead the people in the Old Testament. In what ways does God lead us today?

11. Why did Abram go to Egypt?

12. After reading about what he told his wife, what do you think about Abram?

13. What kind of people did God choose to use to fulfill His plan?

14. Abram and Sarai had great faith to pick up and follow God. Who are the examples of great faith in your life and why are they examples?

What lessons can we learn from this reading for our personal faith and life?

WEEK 5: Abram and Lot – We Are Family!   Genesis 13 – 15

1. Why did Abram and Lot separate?

2. Where did each live?

3. Again, what did God promise Abram?

4. What happened to Lot?

5. What did Abram do when he heard about Lot's trouble?

6. When we talk about the people in Abram's household, about how many are we talking?

7. How did the king of Sodom react to what Abram did?

8. What did the king of Sodom ask for?

9. Why did Abram respond the way he did to the king of Sodom's request?

10. How was the Lord appearing to Abram?

11. About what was Abram worried?

12. How did God respond to his concerns?

13. What did God tell Abram when he fell into the deep sleep?

14. Why is this covenant important?

What lessons can we learn from this reading for our personal faith and life?

WEEK 6: Hagar & Ishmael – A Complicated Family   Genesis 16 – 17

1. God kept telling Abram he woiuld have more descendants than he can count, but Abram had no children and his wife was old and (so far) barren. Why do you think Sarai gives her slave to have children for her?

2. What happened because of Sarai's decision?

3. When Hagar ran away from Sarai how did God resolve the problem?

4. Describe the kind of man that Hagar's son would be.

5. Why do you think it's so hard for people to trust that God really knows what's best for them?

6. God told Abram to walk before Him faithfully and be blameless. What does it mean to be *blameless*?

7. Why did God change Abram and Sarai's names?

8. What was the covenant God made with Abraham?

9.   What was the covenant of circumcision?

10. How did Abraham respond to God telling him that he and Sarah would have a child at 90 and 100 years old?

11. What did Abraham ask God regarding his first son, Ishmael?

12. How did God respond?

13. What would be the difference between God's relationship with Ishmael and with Isaac?

14. So, what was the beginning of the fulfilling of the covenant?

What lessons can we learn from this reading for our personal faith and life?

WEEK 7: The Jacob Saga   Genesis 29-30:22, 32

Isaac was born and both Ishmael and Isaac were blessed by God with many descendants. Isaac married Rebekah. They had two sons, Esau (hairy) and Jacob (schemer or trickster). Esau was a skillful hunter enjoying the outdoors while Jacob preferred staying indoors. Esau sold his birthright to his brother for a pot of stew and later Jacob and his mother, Rebekah, tricked Isaac into giving the family blessing to Jacob instead of the oldest son, Esau.

1. Jacob was sent to Laban (Rebekah's brother) in Paddan Aram to find a wife and get away from his brother's murderous threats. How did he first meet Rachel?

2. If Rachel was the daughter of Jacob's mother's brother, how are Jacob and Rachel related? Do you find this relationship odd or interesting in any way?

3. Why did Jacob stay with Laban? Did he work for free?

4. Some marriage traditions in the Old Testament had three stages. First, a contract between the groom and the bride's father is made. Then, when the groom pays what is in the contract, the union can be consummated. After the consummation there is a wedding feast that can last up many days. Outline the parts of Jacob and Rachel's marriage.

5. Why did Laban say he tricked Jacob and gave him Leah instead of Rachel?

6. How do you explain Jacob not noticing that Leah was with him a whole night?

7. How long did Jacob have to wait to take Rachel as his bride?

8. As you read about Jacob's children, fill in the chart in Appendix A in the back.

9. What were the messengers supposed to tell Esau?

10. How did Esau respond? Why was Jacob afraid to meet his brother?

11. What was Jacob's prayer about? What was he saying to God?

12. What did Jacob want from God in order to let the "man" go after wrestling with him?

13. What does it mean to you to be blessed by God?

14. How did this moment change Jacob? What does his new name mean for us and God's plan?

15. After reading about Jacob (schemer or trickster), describe his character. What kind of man was he?

What lessons can we learn from this reading for our personal faith and life?

WEEK 8: Joseph, the Dreamer

Genesis 37, 39, 41, 50:15-21

Jacob and Esau reconciled. God blessed Jacob and confirmed his new name, Israel.

1. For what reasons (give at least 3) did Joseph's brothers not like him?

2. What was the general message of the dreams?

3. Why were the brothers upset about the dreams?

4. What do you think about what Joseph's brothers wanted to do to him?

5. Which, if any of Joseph's brothers, had a conscience about his/their behavior?

6. How did this change what happened?

7. God uses people to complete His plan of salvation. How is God using Joseph's life?

8. What did the brothers do to cover up their bad behavior?

9. Joseph was in prison in Egypt for 2 years... waiting. If you put yourself in his spot, what are you thinking?

10. What happened with Joseph and Potiphar's wife?

11. What small kindnesses did God show Joseph when in prison?

12. While in prison, Joseph interpreted the dreams of the cupbearer and the baker who had angered the king. Pharaoh heard about this. Describe the Pharaoh's dreams.

13. Joseph didn't try to make himself important to Pharaoh. He was using the gifts God gave him and it just happened in God's time and for God's reason. What lesson can you learn from that?

14. How did God use what happened to Joseph in His plan of salvation for his family and for us?

What lessons can we learn from this reading for our personal faith and life?

WEEK 9: We are Slaves, Dear Moses.   Exodus 1 – 3

During the famine Joseph's brothers went to Egypt for grain. They didn't recognize him so he devised a plan to test them using his youngest brother, Benjamin, so that he could reunite with his family. Once reunited, Joseph brought his brothers and his father to Egypt to take care of them. Before he died, Jacob blessed Joseph's sons, Ephraim and Manasseh, making them two of the 12 tribes of Israel. About 400 years later...

1.   When the leadership changes, everything changes. What happened to change the fate of the Israelites in Egypt?

2.   What emotion was the motivation behind the king's comment, "we must deal shrewdly with them?"

3.   What does *oppress* mean? What was done to oppress the Israelites? (Use your own words.)

4.   How did Moses get into the Pharaoh's household?

5.   At some point Moses had a change of heart. What happened to bring that about?

6.   Where did Moses end up going and what did he end up doing?

7.   It often looks like the "bad guys" are in charge of the world. The pharaoh appeared to be a bad guy to the Israelites, but when we look at the bigger picture what do we see?

8.   When we are having a hard time understanding the world, what should we do?

9. How did God get Moses' attention? Don't you wish God was that obvious with us today?

10. What were the two reasons Moses gave God for why he couldn't do what God was asking?

11. We see ourselves differently than God sees us. How does God see Moses differently than Moses sees Moses?

12. God hasn't spoken to us through a burning bush in some time. How does God speak to us today?

13. God will work through us and give us strength, wisdom, and courage to fulfill His purpose, but we are often more concerned with our purpose. What can we do to focus more on His purpose?

What lessons can we learn from this reading for our personal faith and life?

WEEK 10: A plague is upon us!   Exodus 7 – 12:30

God gave Moses many signs that he was the man for the job, so Moses went back to Egypt. He and Aaron spoke to Pharaoh, but he would not listen and made their work harder. God, however, promised to deliver the Israelites from slavery.

1. God explained how the plagues were to be a part of His plan to free His people. In your own words, explain the basic plan.

2. When Moses and Aaron went to Pharaoh, he asked them to perform a miracle. What were they to do?

3. List the ten plagues and a brief description of each.

4. The last plague was the worst for the Egyptians. What were the Israelites to do so that the angel of death would pass over their house?

5. God told them and their descendants to commemorate their salvation from this plague every year. What is the name of this festival the Jews still celebrate today? On what day of the year is it celebrated?

6. How and when do we Christians commemorate or celebrate this festival?

What lessons can we learn from this reading for our personal faith and life?

WEEK 11: The Dramatic Exit   Exodus 12:31 – 15:21

1. How long did the Israelites live as slaves in Egypt?

2. The Lord said to Moses, "Consecrate to me every firstborn male." What does *consecrate* mean?

3. Why would Pharaoh suddenly change his mind about the Israelites? What realization did he have?

4. Even after everything that happened, the people had trouble trusting God to deliver them. This lack of trust was the beginning of a common theme in the relationship between God and His people and something we constantly need to be reminded of today. What did the people immediately assume when they saw the army marching after them?

5. How did Moses respond?

6. What did the Israelites have to be afraid of?

7. Give an example of what might happen (or has happened) in your life that would make you think God is not "on your side" or isn't working in your best interest?

8. What does it mean for people to *fear* the Lord?

9. How did the people respond after crossing the Red Sea?

10. Choose a main theme for each section of the song in verses 1b-18 that describe that section. What is each section about? What is the whole song about?

11. What are some of the things we do today to acknowledge the wonderful things God has done and continues to do for us every day?

12. What do you think would be a proper way to thank and praise the Lord?

What lessons can we learn from this reading for our personal faith and life?

WEEK 12: Wandering in the Wilderness   Exodus 15:22 – 18

1. What was the first thing Israel did when they got to the waters of Marah?

2. What promise did God make to them there?

3. What was the second complaint of the Israelites?

4. How did God respond to their grumbling?

5. Why do you think they were not to keep any of what they gathered until morning?

6. How long did the Israelites eat the manna?

7. Why was Moses upset when the people complained of no water?

8. What did God tell Moses to do to get water for the people?

9. Why do you think God wants Moses to do these things in front of the people?

10. What was going to happen to the Amalekites for fighting against God's people?

11. What was Jethro's relationship to Moses?

12. What advice did Jethro give Moses about how he was leading the people?

13. People are often offended when somebody gives them advice. How did Moses respond?

14. How do you usually respond when somebody offers their thoughts on something you're thinking or doing?

What lessons can we learn from this reading for our personal faith and life?

WEEK 13: Rules, Rules, Rules   Exodus 19, 20, 32, 40

1. Look back or think back to God's covenant with Abraham. What was it?

2. In your own words, explain what God told Moses to tell the people of Israel.

3. Why did the Lord choose to come to Moses in a cloud?

4. Why do you think God wanted the people to trust Moses?

5. Why did God have so many rules for the people and tell them not to even touch the base of the mountain or they would die?

6. Nobody likes rules, but we all live by them. List two rules your parents have given you that you don't like. Why do you think they have those rules?

7. God gave rules too. They are to help us remain close to Him and make better choices about how we live and treat our fellow man. List each commandment. After each commandment tell why it's a good rule.

8. In chapters 21-24 God gives laws about slaves, restitution, social justice, the Sabbath, and festivals. He promises that they will conquer the land of Canaan, and confirms the covenant. In chapters 25-31 He describes how the tabernacle should be made, who should help make it, and why the Sabbath is important. What were the people doing while God was giving all this information to Moses?

9. What did Moses say to God when He grew angry at the people for their bad behavior?

10. What was Aaron's excuse to Moses for letting the people turn away from God?

11. The people got to work making the tabernacle and the priestly garments in chapters 32-39, and finally the tabernacle was erected. What was the *tabernacle* and what was its purpose?

What lessons can we learn from this reading for our personal faith and life?

WEEK 14: Follow God – It's a Good Thing   Deuteronomy 29 – 31

The book of Leviticus (Levi) is a guide for the Levites, the priests, the sons of Aaron. The book of Numbers is a more detailed account of the Israelites as they wandered through the wilderness and explains which land in Canaan will go to which tribe, and which towns will be given to the Levites within each tribal area. In the beginning of Deuteronomy, Moses prepares the Israelites for their entrance into Canaan, the promised land, reminding them of their covenant with God and what He has told them.

1. What did Moses remind the people that God has done for them while waiting?

2. What were the terms of the covenant? Be sure to use your own words.

3. Why did God want the people to follow the covenant? What's in it for them?

4. When God destroys a city or the land people ask why? Why did He do that?

5. What were the blessings for the people when they followed God and His commands?

6. What were the consequences if the people didn't follow God and His commands?

7. What does God ultimately want of His people?

8. How old was Moses when they reached the Promised Land?

9. Who commissioned Joshua to be the next leader and how did it happen?

10. Following in the footsteps of Moses would be very intimidating. What did God say to Joshua to encourage him?

11. What are some of your fears?

12. How do you deal with your fear?

13. Just before Moses died, God reminded him of why he would not be entering the promised land. Why was that?

What lessons can we learn from this reading for our personal faith and life?

WEEK 15: Rahab, A Spy's Best Friend   Joshua 2 – 4

Moses dies and Joshua takes over as leader of the Israelites. The reason the Israelites need to be courageous is that the land promised by God is occupied and they will need to remove them from it. God, however, will be with them wherever they go.

1. Who was Rahab and what was her profession?

2. What did Rahab do that was unexpected?

3. What did she ask the spies to do?

4. What did they promise her?

5. How was Rahab connected to Jesus?

6. Briefly retell the story of Rahab in your own words.

7. What do you think would have happened to Rahab had she been caught by the king of Jericho?

8. What situations might people face today where it's dangerous for them to do what is right in the eyes of God?

9. When you think about your future, what's the scariest thing you might face?

10. How did God tell the Israelites to cross the Jordan River?

11. How would they know God is with them?

12. What were the 12 stones used for and what would be their purpose in the future?

What lessons can we learn from this reading for our personal faith and life?

WEEK 16: Victory over Jericho!   Joshua 5 – 6

1. Why were the Amorites afraid of the Israelites?

2. Why did the men need to be re-circumcised?

3. Why did the manna stop?

4. God didn't literally hand cities over. His people had a part in the plan. What did the Lord tell Joshua to do to overtake the city of Jericho?

5. What went with the people to show that God was with them?

6. If you were in battle and were told by your leader to do this, what would your first reaction be?

7. What are *devoted* things?

8. What might the danger be in the people keeping the riches?

9. What would be done with those things? Is that fair? Why or why not?

10. What were they to do with ALL the people and animals in the city?

11. What do you think about them having to do what they did with all the living things?

12. How did meeting the two spies change Rahab's life?

13. What oath did Joshua pronounce?

What lessons can we learn from this reading for our personal faith and life?

WEEK 17: A Few Good Judges: Deborah   Judges 1 – 2, 4

The Hebrew slaves were led by Moses to the border of the promised land and then by Joshua and Caleb for the conquest of the Canaanites. Occasionally and temporarily, judges were raised up by God to lead the people through troubled times. Twelve judges guided the Israelites for about 325 years: Othniel, Ehud, Shamgar, Deborah, Gideon, Tola, Jair, Jephthah, Ibzan, Elon, Abdon, and Samson. Some were faithful to God, most were not.

1. After Joshua died, who did God say was supposed to fight the Canaanites?

2. These battles were not as simple as Joshua's first. Which of the battles did they not win?

3. Why do you think they won all those battles?

4. What did the tribe of Manasseh do (or not do) that displeased God?

5. What was the result of displeasing God in this way?

6. What did the angel tell the people was the problem with what they were doing?

7. After Joshua died God gave other judges. What was wrong with these (or most of these) judges?

8. God decided to let the people remain in their land to test the Israelites. What was He going to test them about?

9. What was Barak supposed to do to defeat Sisera?

10. What was his response?

11. What was his punishment for not following God's plan?

12. How was Sisera killed?

13. As God said through Deborah, who got the credit for killing him?

What lessons can we learn from this reading for our personal faith and life?

WEEK 18: A Few Good Judges: Gideon   Judges 6 – 8

1. Yet again, the Israelites did evil in the sight of the Lord. What was the result of that betrayal of the covenant?

2. What did the prophet say?

3. What was the question Gideon asked the angel while out threshing wheat?

4. It seems a fair question. We hear of the miracles of God, but life is full of difficulty. What was the angel's response?

5. Gideon's response was similar to that of Moses. What did he say and what emotion(s) is/are at work here?

6. Even though an angel is there talking to him, Gideon was not sure. What interaction did he then have with the angel?

7. Why do you think God wanted a small army?

8. Describe how they defeated the Midianites.

9. What was Gideon's ephod?

10. What did the people do after Gideon died?

11. Why do you think it was hard for the people of Israel to truly trust God?

12. Why do you think it's hard for you and all people to truly trust God to know what is best? Why do we turn our back on Him over and over again?

13. In your own words, describe what happened with the people after Gideon died.

What lessons can we learn from this reading for our personal faith and life?

WEEK 19: Samuel – Can You Hear Me Now?   1 Samuel 1 – 4

Twelve judges guided the Israelites for about 325 years. During this time, Ruth followed her mother-in-law, Naomi, to Bethlehem after her husband died. She married Boaz (son of Rahab), and they had a son who was the great-grandfather of David.

1. How was Hannah being bullied?

2. Hannah was overcome with grief about her problem. What did she do about it?

3. When Hannah could take it no more she made a promise to God. What was Hannah's promise?

4. Why did Hannah name her son Samuel?

5. What did it mean to be dedicated to the Lord?

6. In what ways do you consider yourself or your life dedicated to the Lord?

7. What does it mean to treat something with contempt?

8. How were Eli's sons treating the Lord's offering with contempt?

9. Paraphrase what the man of the Lord said to Eli. Why was God angry with them?

10. In what ways do we, in the world, despise and disrespect Him?

11. What was the result of their actions?

12. Eli gave Samuel some great advice about what to do after God called him. What was it?

13. In what ways do you think Eli's advice can be applied to your life?

14. How was the ark of the covenant captured by the Philistines?

15. How did Eli die?

What lessons can we learn from this reading for our personal faith and life?

WEEK 20: But We Want a KING!   1 Samuel 8 – 10

While the ark of the covenant was with the Philistines things did not go well for them, so they put it on a cart with guilt offerings of gold and sent it back to the Israelites. Samuel reminded the Israelites to put away their false gods and follow the one true God with all their hearts. He was a judge for Israel his whole life.

1. Samuel made his sons judges over Israel, what happened with them?

2. Sometimes people say that it's okay to do something they know is wrong because everybody else is doing it. Sometimes people convince themselves that they have a good reason for doing what they know is wrong. Why do you think that it is so hard for people to do what is right?

3. What did the Israelites ask Samuel to give them (that the rest of the world has)?

4. If the people want a king, God will give them one but what was God's warning to them through Samuel?

5. What was the reason the people give for wanting a king?

6. Based on what you've read, describe the kind of person Saul was.

7. Saul was going about his business with no idea of God's plans for him. What did God tell Samuel to do?

8. Prophets, priests, and kings are considered anointed by God. A priest ceremonially pours aromatic or holy oil on their head. After Samuel anointed Saul and told him what was going to happen, what do you think Saul thought?

9. God prepares us all for the tasks He has for us. Saul did not ASK to become king. God CHOSE him. What did Samuel tell Saul would happen to help him realize that God was with him?

10. Describe the process of choosing king Saul.

11. How would you feel if somebody told you that you were going to be chosen king and you would have to listen to God and lead a nation of people?

12. Describe how Saul looked.

13. We will always come up against resistance when doing what God asks of us. What happened almost immediately after Saul was hailed by the people?

14. How have you experienced similar resistance when doing what you know is right?

What lessons can we learn from this reading for our personal faith and life?

WEEK 21: Goodbye Saul, Hello David   1 Samuel 15 – 17

As the Israelites' first king and with the help of God, Saul defeated the Ammonites, Samuel reminded the Israelites to serve the Lord faithfully, Saul fought the Philistines, and then he made a mistake. He became impatient and did not follow God's command that only priests (Samuel) sacrifice. He was told by Samuel that is kingdom would not continue.

1. What exactly did God tell Saul to do to the Amalekites?

2. What three things did Saul do to displease God?

3. Why did God regret making Saul king?

4. Where and why was Saul gone when Samuel went to find him?

5. How did Saul respond when told of his poor choices?

6. Some may say that it was cruel for God to reject Saul after he repented of his sin but God did not reject Saul as a child of His, but as the king or leader of his people. Saul rejected God. What did Saul do that leads to this conclusion?

7. Where did God send Samuel to find a new king?

8. Why was Samuel afraid to go?

9. Remember what it means to consecrate somebody. Why would that be done before a sacrifice?

10. After being anointed, what gift did the Lord give David so that he would be a great king?

11. What was God's plan to get David into the service of Saul?

12. How did Goliath challenge the Israelites? What did he want them to do?

13. What did David say to the Philistines to show that he had more confidence in God than fear of Goliath?

14. Knowing everything that was taking place, what would have been the wisest thing for Saul to do now?

What lessons can we learn from this reading for our personal faith and life?

WEEK 22: The Man After God's Heart   2 Samuel 5 – 7

David and Saul's son, Jonathan, were great friends. God didn't throw Saul off the throne, but God's favor now rested on David. Saul became jealous of David and tried to use him and his success for his own glory. Saul told all of his servants and family to kill David, but Jonathan warned his friend. Saul chased David around the country and twice David spared his life. Saul killed the Lord's priests for supporting David, and after Samuel died, met with a witch/medium to get advice from Samuel. Things did not go well for Saul on the battlefield and after losing everything in a battle with the Philistines, he fell on his sword. David mourned both Saul and Jonathan.

1. Finally, after 14 years, David officially became king of Israel and Judah. What did he do next?

2. What is the City of David?

3. David is known as the man "after God's own heart." What does that mean?

4. What did he do when he wanted to defeat the Philistines that showed he was a man after God's own heart?

5. Why was Uzzah immediately killed when he touched the ark of God? Why can't somebody touch the ark?

6. Why did David not want the ark of God in Jerusalem?

7. Saul had given his daughter, Michal, to David as a wife. Why did Michal say she was angry with David?

8. What was his response to her anger?

9. Summarize God's promise to David.

10. When we pray, we usually ask God for things. Briefly describe the different things David spoke to God about.

11. When you pray what do you pray?

12. Write a brief prayer that you can say every night.

What lessons can we learn from this reading for our personal faith and life?

WEEK 23: Good King – Bad Choices   2 Samuel 11 – 12, Psalm 51

David was devoted to following God and a very successful king.

1. Summarize the story of David and Bathsheba.

2. Once David found out who Bathsheba was, he broke two commandments. Which two and how?

3. David must have known that asking someone to get Bathsheba for him was the wrong thing to do. Why do you think he did it anyway?

4. How do you think this story would have played out if Uriah had gone home to Bathsheba and it was assumed the baby was his?

5. Give examples from the reading that describe the kind of man Uriah was.

6. Give a list of the terrible things David did to cover his sin from the moment he saw Bathsheba to the message he sent for Joab.

7. As is always the case, a sin affects more people than just the sinner. Who else did David's sin affect?

8. Nathan spoke to David about a man who had sinned. Why do you think David didn't realize that what he had done was wrong?

9. How did Nathan help David realize his sin?

10. After all was said and done, how many and which of the commandments did David break?

11. Repenting doesn't remove consequences. What was God's first consequence to David for his actions?

12. In what ways do you think God's punishment fair or unfair?

13. David and Bathsheba had another son. What was the special name God gave him?

14. Psalm 51 was written by David after this experience. What does it tell you about what he was thinking or feeling?

What lessons can we learn from this reading for our personal faith and life?

WEEK 24: Wise–for–a–While King Solomon   1 Kings 1 – 3, 6

After David's sin against God, things didn't go as well as they had before. He had trouble with his older sons. Amnon raped his half-sister, Tamar, and Absalom (Tamar's brother) killed him and ran away. Later Absalom conspires against his father to become king. Absalom is killed and David mourns the son he loved.

1. In your opinion, what are some pros and cons to being a king?

2. Who decided Adonijah would be king? Whose support did Adonijah get? Who did he forget to ask?

3. Solomon would not be king because he wanted to be, or thought he deserved to be. Why did David choose Solomon to be king?

4. What did David do about the problem of who would be king?

5. What did Adonijah realize when he found out that Solomon was on the throne to make him so afraid?

6. What warning did Solomon give his brother?

7. What advice did David give Solomon before he died?

8. What kind of spiritual advice does your mom or dad give you?

9.   How did Solomon follow the final directions of his father regarding Joab and Shimei?

10. When God went to Solomon in a dream and told him to ask for anything he wanted, for what did Solomon ask?

11. When you really need serious advice to whom do you go? Friend(s)? Family member(s)? Pastor? Teacher? Somebody else? Why do you choose that person?

12. At the end of the dream God told Solomon what He has told the people of Israel and all of the judges and kings before him. What was it?

13. How do we benefit from the wisdom of Solomon today?

14. Since the time of Moses, where did God "dwell" all this time and what would a temple mean?

What lessons can we learn from this reading for our personal faith and life?

WEEK 25: And Then There Were Two   1 Kings 11 – 12

Solomon has now built the temple and his palace. He brought the ark into the temple and the glory of the Lord filled the house of the Lord and Solomon said a prayer of dedication. Solomon was known around the world for his wisdom and the great wealth he collected.

1. What was Solomon's great weakness?

2. God appeared to Solomon twice and he was given much, but he eventually did what other judges and kings did to lose God's favor. What did he do?

3. What was the result of his choices?

4. Who were Solomon's adversaries?

5. What were the books in which Solomon wrote his reflections or thoughts? What was each about?

6. What was the name of Solomon's son who would succeed him as king?

7. Why was Jeroboam a problem for Rehoboam?

8. To what two groups did Rehoboam go for advice and what was the difference in that advice?

9.   Why do you think the advice from each group was so different?

10. How do you define "good" advice?

11. When somebody gives you advice, how do you determine if you want to follow it?

12. What did God (through Ahijah) say was going to happen to the kingdom of Israel?

13. Who were now the leaders of each of the two kingdoms?

14. What is *spiritual compromise*? Where do you see it in the world today?

What lessons can we learn from this reading for our personal faith and life?

WEEK 26: Elijah and His Chariot   1 Kings 17 – 19, 2 Kings 2

Solomon's son, Rehoboam was the next king, but was rejected by much of Israel except the tribes of Judah and Benjamin. Israel chose Jeroboam. So there were two kingdoms: Israel (north) and Judah (south). There was continual war between the two kings until they both died. Ahab was reigning in Israel when Elijah predicted a drought.

1. Even though God already told him the woman would feed him, what was Elijah's attitude when asking the widow for food and drink?

2. What did the Lord promise the woman through Elijah?

3. What did the woman learn about God from Elijah?

4. What did the king call Elijah when they met?

5. What was Elijah's response to the king? What was the king and his family doing that upset God?

6. What did Elijah ask the people? What was he talking about?

7. What did Elijah tell the people to do to challenge the prophets of Baal?

8. What happened to the prophets of Baal?

9. Elijah had a rough time after the whole prophets of Baal incident. For what did he pray?

10. After God gave Elijah a break, what did He tell him to do?

11. What did Elisha ask Elijah to give him?

12. Did Elisha get what he asked for? How did Elijah tell him he would know if he got it?

13. People don't often see that they've gotten what they've asked for, but in this case, Elisha did. Has anything happened in your life where you have seen a prayer answered?

14. Things don't happen randomly with God. There's a plan. As you've read the Old Testament, what do you think God's message is for you and all people?

What lessons can we learn from this reading for our personal faith and life?

WEEK 27: Oops! Conquered by Assyria

2 Kings 17 – 19

The people of God continue in two groups: Israel (north) and Judah (south) and things aren't going well for either of them, but especially Israel. From the time Jeroboam became king he created idols and led Israel to sin. Eventually, God has had enough.

1. God made a covenant with His people but a covenant is not a one-way promise and they broke it time and again. What was the covenant?

2. Who was the last king of Israel and to where was Israel exiled?

3. List 5 ways the Israelites sinned against God, breaking the covenant.

4. Who did God use to warn the Israelites?

5. In what ways do we imitate "the nations around" us and their culture even though the Lord tells us not to do as they do?

6. What happened to the people of Israel when they were rejected by God due to their inability to keep their side of the covenant and their rejection of God?

7. List three things that your friends think are acceptable but God does not.

8. What ended up happening to the kingdom of Israel?

9. What was it about Hezekiah that redeemed the kingdom of Judah?

10. What did Hezekiah give the king of Assyria to leave Judah alone?

11. How did the Assyrian commander taunt the people of Judah?

12. How are Christians today taunted for following God?

13. How did God respond through Isaiah to the taunting? What will happen to the Assyrian commander in his own country?

14. In prayer Hezekiah asked the Lord to deliver His people for a specific reason. What was it?

What lessons can we learn from this reading for our personal faith and life?

WEEK 28: The Trouble with Kings   2 Kings 21 – 23

Many times God warned the people that He would remove them from His presence. Finally, because of their constant rejection of God and refusal to follow Him, He allowed the king of Assyria to capture the Israelites and take them to Assyria. The tribes of Judah and Benjamin were all that was left of God's people.

1. Give three examples that describe the kind of king Manasseh was.

2. What did God say would happen because of how Manasseh led the kingdom of Judah?

3. What is a *remnant*? What does it mean in this context?

4. Knowing what the people did, what do you think about God's response?

5. What have they been doing or what do they keep doing that angers God?

6. How long did Amon reign?

7. Amon's son, Josiah took over after the assassination. How was he different from his father?

8. What was Josiah's mission with regard to the temple?

9.   What was found in the temple?

10. What did Josiah discover about the book?

11. When they asked the Lord what would happen since they didn't follow His law, what did He say?

12. How did Josiah respond to what God told the people of their consequence?

13. How was Josiah different from any other king?

14. Even though Josiah had a heart for following God, how did He feel about the people of Judah?

What lessons can we learn from this reading for our personal faith and life?

WEEK 29: Judah, Captive in Babylon   2 Kings 24 – 25, Jeremiah 50 – 51

For a while, Judah and its kings did right in the eyes of the Lord. Eventually, however, they too rejected Him.

1. Now God had said He was going to remove Judah from his presence just as he promised. How did He say that would come about?

2. What was the Lord not willing to forgive?

3. What does it mean to "do evil in the eyes of the Lord?"

4. Who was the king of Babylon when Jehoiakim was king of Judah?

5. How did Jehoiachin behave while his city was besieged by the Babylonians?

6. What did the king of Babylon do with everything when he took Jerusalem? What was left?

7. How was Zedekiah related to Jehoiachin and how did he become king?

8. When the Babylonians took Zedekiah and Jerusalem, what did they do to his family?

9. As the Babylonians removed the people, what did they do with the temple?

10. What happened to all of the priests?

11. Why do you think the king of Babylon treated Jehoiachin well as long as he lived?

12. Jeremiah had a message from God to the Babylonians. Briefly, what would happen to them?

13. Why was God going to do all that to the Babylonians?

What lessons can we learn from this reading for our personal faith and life?

WEEK 30: Esther – For a Time Like This   Esther 3 – 7

Esther is the story of how God used a Jewish woman living in exile in Babylon. Mordecai, her cousin, raised her as she had no parents. The king, Xerxes, had trouble with his current wife who refused to attend a banquet, so he decided to search for a new wife. Esther, not telling the king she was a Jew, won his favor and was chosen.

1. What was Haman's problem with the Jews?

2. How did Haman convince the king to have the Jews killed?

3. How did Mordecai use his connection with Esther in this situation?

4. How did Esther respond to what she heard about the edict? How do you think she felt?

5. What does Mordecai tell Esther to change her mind?

6. God's plan will be accomplished whether you participate or not and we never know how God intends to use us. How do those words inspire you?

7. What is Esther's petition to the king?

8. Why do you think Haman felt such rage against Mordecai?

9. Haman had reached great status and position with the king. Why did none of that make him happy?

10. What do you think about Haman's wife's suggestion?

11. Sometimes we do good things to bring attention to ourselves. What did Mordecai do that didn't bring attention to himself that the king wanted to reward him for?

12. Things were not going the way Haman expected. How are his plans all backfiring?

13. What happened at the banquet and what was the result for Haman?

14. While Esther spoke up about Haman there was still the problem of the edict to kill all Jews. The king's edict cannot be revoked. How will they fix this problem? What did the new edict allow?

What lessons can we learn from this reading for our personal faith and life?

WEEK 31: Daniel and the Fiery Furnace Trio   Daniel 1 – 3, 6

Daniel is the story of a Jewish man living in exile in Babylon.

1. How did Daniel end up in the Babylonian king's service?

2. What does *integrity* mean? Give two examples of what someone with integrity would do.

3. Why did Daniel not want to eat the food the king assigned to him?

4. According to the king's official, what would the problem be if Daniel didn't eat?

5. What was Daniel's plan to fix that and how did it turn out?

6. What did the king ask the astrologers that seemed like a trick question?

7. How was the mystery revealed to Daniel?

8. How did Daniel give credit where credit is due? Why did Daniel say God revealed the dream to him?

9. The Jews in Babylon had to change many things when taken into captivity. What would they not do?

10. Give three examples from your life when you do things you know are not God pleasing.

11. What changed for Nebuchadnezzar because of what they did?

12. Why didn't the administrators and satraps like Daniel? What did they do about it?

13. Why do you think the king liked Daniel?

14. How did the king react when he saw that Daniel was not killed by the lions?

What lessons can we learn from this reading for our personal faith and life?

WEEK 32: Home Sweet Home   Ezra 1, 3 – 4

God is constantly giving his people another chance. About 70 years pass before the exiles are allowed to return to Jerusalem. God decided it was time to rebuild.

1. What was Cyrus, king of Persia, moved by God to do?

2. What were the local people to do to help the exiles returning to Jerusalem?

3. What was Cyrus going to do with the items Nebuchadnezzar confiscated?

4. Why did the people choose to rebuild the altar first?

5. Why do you think they built what goes inside the temple before the building itself?

6. Why do you think some of the people were crying while others were celebrating?

7. What's the problem with the "enemies" of Judah and Benjamin offering to help rebuild the temple? After all, it's just help…

8. How do people in the world usually react when somebody stands up for what they believe?

9. What resistance did the people face when rebuilding?

10. Share two examples you have seen where people standing up for God's ways meet with resistance, are ridiculed or persecuted in public.

11. In your own words, describe what the letter to King Artaxerxes said.

12. What happened to the rebuilding effort because of this letter?

What lessons can we learn from this reading for our personal faith and life?

WEEK 33: A Time to Rebuild   Ezra 5 – 7

1. What did the governor of Trans-Euphrates ask the people who were rebuilding the temple?

2. Why might the governor be concerned about rebuilding this temple?

3. Why do you think his request of the king is fair or unfair?

4. What did King Darius find in the archives?

5. What did the decree say regarding interfering with the rebuild?

6. What should happen to anyone who doesn't follow the decree?

7. How was the temple rededicated?

8. Why do you think the people of the Old Testament celebrated by sacrificing animals?

9. How long did it take Ezra to get to Jerusalem?

10. What did the letter from Artaxerxes to Ezra say?

11. What are the people to do with all artifacts that were taken by the Babylonians?

12. What is Ezra allowed to teach the people?

13. The people of God are back in Jerusalem. How might these people be different (or not) from those He escorted out of Egypt?

14. Briefly tell the story God's relationship with the Israelites in the space below.

_____

_____

_____

_____

_____

_____

_____

_____

_____

_____

_____

_____

_____

_____

_____

APPENDIX A – The 12 Sons of Jacob

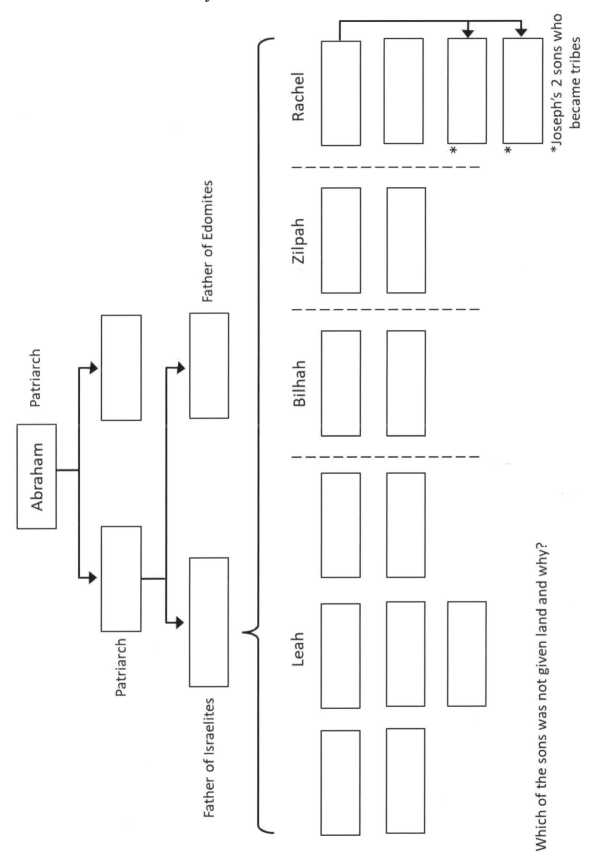

APPENDIX B – Project Information

Old Testament Timeline

The Old Testament takes place over a long period of time and it's difficult to understand the steadfastness of God and his promises without some context. This timeline project allows students to see the story of God's relationship with his people in a succinct way. The goal of this project is for students to briefly summarize each of the 33 events as they learn them each week.

Here are some tips:

- One option would be for students in pairs or groups to create a visual timeline down a hallway for people to see and learn about the Old Testament. Each student or pair of students would have a different responsibility as they rotate through each event.
- Have students create a section for every major event read about or discussed. There are 33. If necessary, a few can be combined.
- To present, have a big reveal on a Wednesday night at the end of the year and have a potluck. After everyone eats students can act like tour guides as they explain their section to others. It would be a night when other midweek students or families can learn about the Old Testament story.
- Another option would be to have students each create their own timeline as they go through the book using the template sample in Appendix B. It can be created by creating columns in a notebook.
- Yet another option would be to have students create a notebook including all the items listed below. They should be able to show and tell the story of God's people in the Old Testament.
- Depending on the number of students in the class, they can work alone, in pairs, or in groups.
- The following items should be included in each timeline event:
  - Title – Be creative, but make sure it fits the event.
  - Biblical reference – Book and chapters
  - No less than 2 and no more than 5 specifically chosen Bible verses that describe the event.
  - Two or three pictures – They can be drawn or taken from the internet.
  - A summary of the event written by students – should be no longer than 1 page.
  - Statement of how this event fits into God's plan of salvation for his people. Examples:
    - God wants to love and so he creates something he can love and gives them a place to live by speaking it into existence.
    - God's creatures choose themselves over him and must suffer the consequences. God forgives them.
    - David loses his way and lets his temptation pull him away from God. He doesn't even see what he's done and it takes Nathan to show him. He repents and God forgives him.
    - The Israelites once again fall away from God and must suffer the consequences, though God does not leave them.

Parents' Role in Projects

It is always great for parents to help their children, as long as they don't help too much. Asking guiding questions is always better than doing something for a child.

	Appropriate Help	Going Too Far
When kids get stuck and ask for help, ask them questions instead of giving them the answers.		
Project Management	Creating a plan or schedule **with** your child. Reminding your child to work on the project according to the schedule.	Creating a plan or schedule **for** your child and working on the project without your child.
Writing or Summarizing	Discussing the pros and cons of what to include and letting your child write the information in their own words.	Choosing information for your child and helping him/her write it.
Choosing Bible Verses	Choosing verses for your child or showing your child "better" verses.	Allowing your child to choose verses and asking questions to help guide.
Choosing Pictures	Taking your child to the library or helping find keywords for an Internet search.	Finding pictures for your child. Doing an Internet search and printing them for your child.
Proofreading	Circling information that needs to be changed (spelling and grammar).	Rewriting for your child. Correcting spelling and grammar for them.
Creating a Book	Discussing the benefits and challenges of how to lay out each page, but allowing your child final choice.	Working on the book for your child or when the child isn't home.
Practicing a Presentation	Acting like an audience.	Helping students present.

APPENDIX C – Timeline Template

Event Title	Biblical Reference	Summary
Noah and the Great Flood	*Genesis 6-8*	*All the world was corrupt except for Noah and his family. God decided to destroy the earth with a huge flood. Noah built a large boat called an ark to save his family and the animals. It rained for 40 days and Noah and his family were on the ark for approximately a year.*

APPENDIX D: The Art of Leading Discussion

TELL ME WHAT YOU KNOW

Leading discussion is an art. Effective discussions can provide a number of positive interactions between teachers and students. They provide teachers with feedback, they support a higher level of thinking which helps develop values and change attitudes, they allow participation in learning, and they give students a chance to hear and share different viewpoints (Schurr, 1995).

There are some tricks of the trade to help teachers become skilled at guiding a discussion to a specific point and that will help create an environment where students will share their thoughts and opinions comfortably. (For more information on teaching confirmation, see my book, *The Art of Teaching Confirmation*.)

Time to Respond—Give students time to think and respond. If the teacher jumps in with a response students will wait until that happens every time which will stifle the discussion.

Encourage Without Giving Too Much—Don't prod students by starting an answer for them and hoping they catch on. This leads them to your conclusion. What you're looking for is *their* input or conclusion.

Speak Less—The point of discussion is to broaden students' thoughts and find out what they think in case they need some guidance or more information. Guide them by asking more questions, not directly sharing your opinions.

Give Your Opinion at the End—If you state your opinion too early, they will agree with you and the discussion will be over. Try to get them to come to a conclusion through leading questions such as:

- Why do you think that?
- I need help clarifying. Can you give me an example?
- What do you mean by…?
- I'd like to hear more about that.
- What about…?
- Does anybody else have something to add?

Sometimes students fall into a predictable pattern where the same vocal students always respond or the group sits looking at you as if you don't speak their language and nobody says a word. If that happens, try a bean bag, a talking stick, or another object that is only used for this purpose.

Ask a question and toss a beanbag to a student to answer it. They can toss it back to you or to another student to respond to the same question or another question. Don't be surprised if at one point somebody says, "Throw it to me!" because they have something to share. If they start talking over each other remind them that the person with the beanbag is the speaker and everyone else listens and thinks.

If students disagree with what another student says, don't be as concerned about whether or not they agree or disagree as to *why* they agree or disagree. One of the goals of a discussion is to help students refine and communicate what they think or believe. We want to give them the opportunity to develop their own thoughts, opinions, and feelings based on what they have learned. However, they are young and again, their logic will be off and their life experience is small, so let them be challenged and see if they figure it out for themselves before you jump in and correct. There's nothing better than watching the wheels turn in the heads of 13 year old kids as they rationalize and realize things they didn't know before. It's after great discussions that they get in the car and keep talking all the way home!

REFERENCES

Wilmington, H. L., *70 Most Important Events in the Bible* (based on the book, Willmington's Guide to the Bible). Tyndale House Publishers, Inc., Wheaton IL, 1987 (online at http://www.angelfire.com/il/lcms/events.html)

The Story (2011), Zondervan Publishers

The Bible, NIV

Biblegateway.com

Laura Langhoff Arndt's big head full of questions.

ABOUT THE AUTHOR

Laura Langhoff Arndt is the woman behind the Carpenter's Ministry Toolbox, a Christian education resource ministry whose goal is to apply current educational research and strategies to congregational education. She dreams of equipping and encouraging pastors, other professional church workers, and volunteers to effectively educate God's children from preschool through adult. Laura is a professional educator with an M.A. in classroom instruction, administrative leadership experience, as well as Director of Christian Education (DCE) certification in the LCMS.

One of her many passions is to visit with both professional and volunteer church educators in person through workshops providing educational resources, support, and encouragement. Learn more at
www.carpentersministrytoolbox.com

Laura lives in Rochester, MN with her husband, Kevin, and two of eight step-children.
She enjoys painting watercolors and riding her bike.

Books by Laura Langhoff Arndt:

The Art of Teaching Confirmation
Old Testament Reading Plan and Workbook (middle and high school)
Gospels and Acts Reading Plan and Workbook (middle school)
Acts and Epistles Reading Plan and Workbook (coming soon)
I Am Jesus' Little Lamb: God's Gifts at Baptism

Made in the USA
Monee, IL
13 August 2021